Our Iceberg Is Melting

What People Are Saying

"*Our Iceberg Is Melting* is superb. It embodies powerful messages that can help a broad audience. It covers all the steps to success in a changing world, from finding the substantial issues, aligning with a potent champion, charting the course, getting buy-in, dealing with those who want no change, and so on."

— CHRIS HAND
CITIGROUP GLOBAL ACCOUNT VICE PRESIDENT
AVAYA CORPORATION

"Never have I read a parable in a business book that took a complex issue like change management and distilled it down into a simple story for all to understand. This is the ideal follow-on to *Leading Change* and *The Heart of Change*. A must-read for anyone dealing with managing change."

— RICHARD J. KOSINSKI
CATEGORY DEVELOPMENT OFFICER
YAHOO, INC.

"*Our Iceberg Is Melting* is fantastic—offbeat, but right on. We should make everyone in Washington, D.C., read it."

— JOHN BATTEN
EXECUTIVE VICE PRESIDENT
TWIN DISC, INC.

"I came across *Our Iceberg Is Melting* in May, ordered and distributed sixty copies in June, evaluated its effect on our change effort, and then ordered five hundred more copies in September. This is a gem."

— HEIDI KING
PROGRAM MANAGER
DEPARTMENT OF DEFENSE

"This is the easiest-to-read yet most informative book I have ever seen. Setting one of management's biggest challenges— 'what problem, I don't see a problem'—in the context of a melting iceberg and a determined penguin was a stroke of sheer genius."

— MICHAEL DIMELOW
DIRECTOR, PRODUCT MARKETING
TTP COMMUNICATIONS PLC

"I have followed Kotter's work for years, respect it greatly, use it with my clients, and know its unique power to help people and organizations perform better. This latest effort—this little penguin tale—is, in my opinion, the best and most useful book he has ever written."

— ALAN FROHMAN
PRESIDENT
FROHMAN ASSOCIATES

"As a result of the book and my sharing it with a few people in the organization, we have moved quickly on several fronts. We are galvanized to go ahead instead of further studying, more organizing, and so on. It is making a difference for us."

— TOM CURLEY
PRESIDENT AND CEO
ASSOCIATED PRESS

"It's a great book. It does an excellent job of communicating in a simple and humorous way the key challenges of leading change. We can easily identify with the characters. It allows a light-hearted discussion of very difficult issues."

— DEB KARSTETTER
EXECUTIVE VICE PRESIDENT
ABD INSURANCE & FINANCIAL SERVICES

"When I was a child in France, I was first introduced to the French classic *The Little Prince*. I reread this marvelous book while in college and many times since as an adult. It is a book that keeps me growing and thinking. I can see *Our Iceberg Is Melting* becoming *The Little Prince* for the twenty-first century."

— STEPHAN BANCEL
GENERAL MANAGER
ELI LILLY, BELGIUM

"My fifteen-year-old daughter saw me reading *Our Iceberg Is Melting,* and when I left the book in the den, she began to read it. When she was done, my wife read it. Afterward, we all talked about it. What I suspect will happen with our family, and especially with our daughter, is that we now have a referent story to use, one that's easy to remember and visually salient, when we discuss issues about change. It has 'stickiness' in that it's hard to forget."

— PETER Z. ORTON, PH.D.
PROGRAM DIRECTOR, SPECIAL PROJECTS
IBM ON DEMAND LEARNING

"In this fast-paced world, with piles of data and written material, this book is a breath of fresh air. It is simple and to the point, easy to read, and filled with many ideas that we can all apply. I found my mind reflecting on the past on one page and thinking about the future on the next."

— EDWARD DAY
EXECUTIVE VICE PRESIDENT
SOUTHERN COMPANY GENERATION

Our Iceberg Is Melting

*Changing and Succeeding
Under Any Conditions*

by

John Kotter

and

Holger Rathgeber

with artwork by Peter Mueller

St. Martin's Press ✽ New York

www.stmartins.com

Library of Congress Cataloging-in-Publication Data

Kotter, John P., 1947–
    Our iceberg is melting : changing and succeeding under any conditions / John Kotter and Holger Rathgeber—1st St. Martin's Press ed.
        p. cm.
    ISBN-13: 978-0-312-36198-3
    ISBN-10: 0-312-36198-X
    1. Organizational change. 2. Organizational effectiveness. 3. Penguins—Fiction. I title

    HD58.8 .K672 2006
    650.1—dc22
                                                                    2006043101

First published in the United States by John Kotter and Holger Rathgeber under the title *Our Iceberg Is Melting: Changing and Succeeding Under Adverse Conditions*

First St. Martin's Press Edition: September 2006

10 9 8 7 6 5 4 3 2

Foreword

By Spencer Johnson, M.D.

Author of **Who Moved My Cheese?**

Coauthor of **The One Minute Manager**

On the surface, this wonderful book appears to be a simple fable that is easy to read and understand. But that is just the tip of the proverbial iceberg.

Working with John Kotter, at the Harvard Business School, I learned that he knows more about changing organizations than anyone, anywhere. Leaders and managers around the world have read his highly respected book, *Leading Change,* and have discovered that using his Eight Steps is the best way to ensure a successful organizational change.

What does that have to do with most of us?

Well, with *Our Iceberg Is Melting,* everyone working in any kind of organization—and that is most people—can now discover how to use the same

Eight Steps, and enjoy more success in these changing times.

Professor Kotter and his equally creative coauthor Holger Rathgeber, let us see how a group of penguins, in adverse conditions, use the steps, seemingly without knowing it.

Whether you work in a business, or the business of life, everyone from CEO's to high school students, can gain from what each takes from this story.

As you enjoy reading what follows, you may want to ask yourself, "What is my 'iceberg,' and how can I use what I discover in the story?"

And then consider sharing it with others you work with. After all, things usually turn out better when everyone is on the same page.

Our Iceberg Is Melting

Welcome

Handle the challenge of change well, and you can prosper greatly. Handle it poorly, and you put yourself and others at risk

All too often people and organizations don't see the need for change. They don't correctly identify what to do, or successfully make it happen, or make it stick. Businesses don't. School systems don't. Nations don't.

We have studied the challenge of change for decades. We know the traps into which even very smart people fall. We know the steps that can assure group success. And we will show you what we have found.

Our method is showing, much more than telling, and showing with the method that has helped more people learn over the centuries than any other single technique: the fable.

Fables can be powerful because they take serious, confusing, and threatening subjects and make them clear and approachable. Fables can be memorable, unlike so much of the information that bombards us today and is forgotten tomorrow. They can stimulate thought, teach important lessons, and motivate anyone—young or old—to use those lessons. In our modern, high-tech world, we can easily forget this simple yet profound truth.

The fable that follows was inspired by John Kotter's award-winning research on how succesful change really happens. All of us encounter the basic issues in the story. Few of us encounter highly effective ways of dealing well with those issues.

If you know much about the setting in which we have placed our story—Antarctica—you'll see that life for our penguins is not exactly as you would find it on a National Geographic documentary. Fables are like that. If you think a fun story with illustrations must be for young children, you'll soon see this book is about real-life problems that frustrate nearly everyone in organizations.

For readers who would prefer to begin by learning about the history of this book, its intellectual underpinnings, the Eight Step change method, or excactly how this fable can help you succeed in an era of change, we have placed that material after the story on page 128. If that doesn't feel needed now, just find a comfortable chair and read on.

Our Iceberg Will Never Melt

Once upon a time a colony of penguins was living in the frozen Antarctic on an iceberg near what we call today Cape Washington.

The iceberg had been there for many, many years. It was surrounded by a sea rich in food. On its surface were huge walls of eternal snow that gave penguins shelter from dreadful winter storms.

As far back as any of the penguins could remember, they had always lived on that iceberg. "This is our home," they would tell you if you could ever find their world of ice and snow. They would also say, quite logically from their perspective, "and this will always be our home."

Where they lived, a waste of energy kills. Everyone in the colony knew they needed to huddle together to survive. So they had learned to depend on each other. They often behaved like a big family (which, of course, can be both good and bad).

The birds were truly beautiful. Called Emperor Penguins, they were the largest of seventeen types of Antarctic animals that seem perpetually to wear tuxedos.

Two hundred sixty-eight penguins lived in the colony. One of them was Fred.

Fred looked and acted much like the others. You would probably describe him as either "cute" or "dignified," unless you really dislike animals. But Fred was different from most penguins in one very important way.

This is Fred.
He is watching
the sea.

Fred was unusually curious and observant.

Other penguins went hunting for creatures in the sea—quite necessary, since there was no other food in Antarctica. Fred fished less and studied the iceberg and the sea more.

Other penguins spent much of their time with friends and relatives. Fred was a good husband and father, but he socialized less than average. He frequently went off by himself to take notes on what he had observed.

You might think that Fred was an odd bird, perhaps the sort of penguin that others did not want to spend time with. But that wasn't really true. Fred was just doing what seemed right to him. As a result, he was becoming increasingly alarmed by what he saw.

Fred had a briefcase stuffed full of observations, ideas, and conclusions. (Yes, a briefcase. This is a fable.) The information was increasingly disturbing. The information was beginning to cry out:

The Iceberg Is Melting and Might Break Apart Soon!!

An iceberg that suddenly collapsed into many pieces would be a disaster for the penguins, especially if it occurred during the winter in a storm. Many of the older and younger birds would surely die. Who could say what all the consequences would be? Like all unthinkable events, there was no plan for how to deal with such a catastrophe.

Fred did not panic easily. But the more he studied his observations, the more he became unnerved.

Fred knew he had to do something. But he was in no position to make any pronouncements or dictate how others should act. He was not one of the leaders of the colony. He wasn't even a son, brother, or father of one of the leaders of the colony. And he had no track record as a credible iceberg forecaster.

Fred also remembered how fellow-penguin Harold had been treated when he once suggested that their home was becoming more fragile. When no one seemed interested, Harold tried to assemble some evidence. His efforts were greeted with:

"Harold, you really do worry too much.
Have a squid, you'll feel better."

"Fragile?! Jump up and down Harold.
Have fifty of us jump up and down at the same time. Does anything happen? Huh?"

"Your observations are fascinating Harold. But they can be interpreted in four very different ways. You see, if one makes the assumption..."

Some birds said nothing, but they began to treat Harold differently. The change was subtle, but Fred had seen it. It was definitely not a change for the better.

Fred found himself feeling rather lonely.

What Do I Do Now?

The colony had a Leadership Council. It was also called the Group of Ten, led by the Head Penguin. (The teenagers had another name for the group, but that's another story.)

Alice was one of the ten bosses. She was a tough, practical bird who had a reputation for getting things done. She was also close to the colony, unlike a few of her peers who were more aloof. Actually all of their breed of penguins look a bit aloof, but they don't all behave that way.

Fred decided that Alice would be less likely to dismiss his story than other more senior penguins. So he went to see her. Alice being Alice, he did not have to schedule an appointment.

Fred told her of his studies and his conclusions. She listened carefully, even though, frankly, she wondered if Fred was having some sort of personal crisis.

But…Alice being Alice, she did not ignore Fred. Instead, she said, skeptically, "Take me to the place that you think most clearly shows the problem."

That "place" was not on the upper surface of the iceberg, where the melting and its consequences were hard to see, but underneath and inside. Fred explained this to Alice. She listened, and not being the most patient of birds, said, "Fine, fine, fine. Let's go."

Penguins are vulnerable when they leap into the water because leopard seals and killer whales hide to catch careless birds. Without going into any unpleasant graphic detail, let's just say that you really don't want to be caught by a killer whale or leopard seal. So when Fred and Alice jumped into the sea, they were instinctively careful.

Below the surface, Fred pointed out fissures and other clear symptoms of deterioration caused by melting. Alice was amazed at how she had managed to ignore these signs.

Alice continued to follow Fred as he turned into a large hole at a sidewall of the iceberg. Through a canal a few meters wide, they swam deep into the heart of the ice, eventually reaching a spacious cave filled with water.

Alice tried to look as if she totally understood what she was seeing, but leadership was her specialty, not the science of icebergs. Fred saw the perplexed look. So when they returned to the surface, he explained.

To make a long story short—

Icebergs are not like ice cubes. The bergs can have cracks inside called canals. The canals can lead to large air bubbles called caves. If the ice melts sufficiently, cracks can be exposed to water, which would then pour into the canals and caves.

During a cold winter, the narrow canals filled with water can freeze quickly, trapping water inside the caves. But as the temperature goes lower and lower, the water in the caves will also freeze. Because a freezing liquid dramatically expands in volume, an iceberg could be broken into pieces.

After a few minutes, Alice began to see why Fred was so deeply concerned. The magnitude of the problem could be…?

This was most definitely not good.

Alice was shaken, though she didn't show it.
Instead, she asked Fred question after question.

"I need to think about what you have shown me,"
she told him, "and then quickly talk with a few
of my fellow leaders." Her mind was already
plotting away.

"I will need your assistance," she told Fred.
"I need you to be prepared to help others see and
feel the problem." After a short pause, she added,
"And be prepared that some birds won't want to see
any problem."

Alice bid Fred good-bye. Fred felt both better
and worse.

Better—He was no longer the only penguin who saw the potential for disaster. He wasn't the only penguin who felt a sense of urgency to do something about the problem.

Worse—He did not yet see any solution. And he did not much like the way Alice had said "be prepared" and "some birds won't want to see any problem."

The awful Antarctic winter was only two months away.

Problem? What Problem?

During the next few days, Alice contacted all members of the Leadership Council, including Louis, the Head Penguin. She asked them to go on the journey she had taken with Fred. Most listened to her. But they were very skeptical. Was Alice having a personal problem, perhaps with her marriage?!

None of those with whom Alice spoke showed any enthusiasm about the idea of swimming into a big dark cave. A few Council members could not even find time to see Alice. They said that they were busy with other important matters. They were dealing with a complaint from a rather loud bird that another penguin was making faces behind his back (a somewhat confusing issue since penguins cannot make faces).

They were also debating whether their weekly meetings should last two or two and one-half hours, a hot issue for those who liked jabbering and those who did not.

Alice asked Louis, the Head Penguin, to invite Fred to the next Leadership Council meeting to present and defend his conclusions. "After what you have told me about him, I am certainly very interested in hearing what Fred has to say," the Head Penguin said—diplomatically.

Louis did not, however, schedule time for a presentation by this relatively unknown penguin who had never before spoken to the group of leaders. But Alice was insistent, reminding her boss that they had to take some risks, "which you have bravely done all your life." That was true, more or less, and Louis was flattered to hear Alice say so (even though her motives were pretty obvious).

The Head Penguin agreed to invite Fred. Alice did.

In preparation for his meeting with the leaders, Fred considered writing a speech in which he would give statistics about the shrinking size of their home, the canals, the caves filled with water, the number of fissures obviously caused by melting, and so on. But when he asked a few of the older members of the colony about the Group of Ten, he learned that:

- Two of the birds on the Leadership Council loved to debate the validity of any statistics. And they loved to debate for hours and hours and hours and hours. These two were the more vocal advocates lobbying for longer meetings.

- One of the Leadership Council members would usually fall asleep—or at least come awfully close—during a long presentation with statistics. His snoring could be disruptive.

- Another bird was very uncomfortable with numbers. He tried to hide his feelings, usually by nodding his head a great deal. All the head nodding tended to annoy some other members of the group, which could lead to bad moods and bickering.

- At least two other Council members made it pretty clear that they did not like to be TOLD much of anything. They saw it as their job to be doing the TELLING.

After much thought, Fred chose an approach to the upcoming meeting that was different from his original plan.

Fred constructed a model of their iceberg. It was four feet by five feet and made of real ice and snow. The construction was not easy for Fred (especially since he had no hands, fingers, and opposable thumbs).

When he was done, Fred knew it was not perfect. But Alice thought it was a very creative idea and definitely good enough to help the leaders begin to see the problem.

The night before the meeting, Fred and his friends moved the model to where the leadership team met, which, unfortunately, was on the highest mountain of the iceberg. Half way up the hill, the grumbling began. "Remind me why I'm doing this" was one of the kinder comments from his friends.

If penguins could grunt and groan, there would have been plenty of both.

The next morning, the leaders were already standing around the model when Fred arrived. Some were engaged in a lively debate. Others looked mystified.

Alice introduced Fred to the group.

Louis started the meeting, as the Head Penguin always did. "Fred, we want to hear about your discovery." Fred bowed respectfully. He could sense openness from Louis and some members of the group. Others seemed neutral. A few made little effort to hide their skepticism.

Fred gathered his thoughts—and courage—and then told the story of his discovery. He explained the methods he had devised to study their home. He described how he had found the deterioration, the open canals, the big exposed cave full of water—all of which had to be caused by melting.

Constantly Fred used the model to orient his audience and illustrate his points. All but one of the Leadership Council penguins moved closer to the model.

When Fred removed the top half of the structure to show the big cave and explain its disastrous impact, you could have heard a snowflake falling on the ground.

When the demonstration was completed, there was silence.

Alice started the discussion by saying, "I saw all this with my own eyes. The cave full of water is huge. It's scary. I saw all the other signs of destruction that must be caused by the melting. We cannot ignore this anymore!"

A few penguins nodded.

One of the Leadership Council members was an older, heavyset bird named NoNo. NoNo was responsible for weather forecasting. There were two theories as to the origin of his name. One was that his great grandfather had been called NoNo. Another theory was that his first words as a baby penguin were not "Ma" or "Pa," but "No, No."

NoNo was accustomed to being blamed for being wrong in his weather forecasts, but this business about the iceberg melting was too much for him. He spoke up, barely able to control his emotions.
"I have regularly reported to this group about my observations of the climate and its effect on our iceberg," he said. "As I have told you before, periods of melting during warm summers are common. During winter, everything returns to normal. What he saw, or *thinks* he saw, is nothing new. There is no reason to worry! Our iceberg is solid and strong, and can withstand such fluctuations!"

Each sentence from NoNo came out louder than the last. If penguins could become red faced, which they can't, he would have been red faced.

When NoNo saw that the support of some of the others was turning in his favor, he pointed to Fred and said dramatically:

"This *junior* bird says melting ice has opened that canal. *But maybe it hasn't.* He says the canal will freeze this winter and trap the water in a big cave. *But maybe it won't!* He says the water in the cave will freeze. *But maybe it will not!* He says freezing water always expands in volume. *But maybe he's wrong!* And even if all he says turns out to be true, is our iceberg really so fragile that freezing water in a cave can break it into dangerously small pieces? *How do we know what he says is not just—a theory? Wild speculation? Fearmongering?!!!*"

NoNo paused, glared at the others, and threw what he hoped was a knock-out punch:

"Can he guarantee that his data and conclusions are 100 percent accurate?"

Four of the birds nodded. One seemed to have become as mad as NoNo.

Alice quietly shot Fred an encouraging look that basically said: things are fine (which she knew was not true), you can handle this (which was not at all clear), now just go ahead and reply calmly (which for her would have been difficult since she wanted to scream, "NoNo, you nitwit!").

Fred said nothing. Alice gave him another encouraging look.

Fred hesitated, then said, "Honestly, no. I cannot give you a guarantee. No, I am not 100 percent sure. But should our melting iceberg break into many pieces, it will be in winter, when it is dark both day and night, when the terrible storms and winds make us most vulnerable. Wouldn't many, many of us die?"

Two of the birds standing near Fred seemed horrified. He looked in their direction and said, "Wouldn't it happen?"

Seeing that most of the Leadership Council still appeared to be very skeptical, Alice gave NoNo a hard look and said: "Imagine parents who lost their children. Imagine them coming to us and asking, 'How could this have happened? What were you doing? Why didn't you foresee this crisis?

It was your job to protect the colony!' What would you tell them? 'Well, yes, sorry. We had heard that there might be a problem, but the information was not 100 percent credible.'"

She paused to let her comments sink in.

"What would we tell them as they stood before us in unspeakable pain? That we had hoped such a tragedy would not happen? That it was not appropriate to act until we were 100 percent sure?"

Again, snowflakes could almost be heard crashing onto the ground.

Beneath her dignified exterior, Alice was so angry she wanted to take the ice model and throw it at NoNo.

Louis, the Head Penguin, noticed a change in the group's mood. He said, "If Fred is correct, then we only have the remaining two months until winter begins to react to this threat."

One of the other penguin leaders said, "We need to form a committee from members of this team to analyze the situation and look into possible solutions."

Many of the birds nodded in agreement.

Another one of them told the group, "Yes, but we must do everything possible so that the colony's routines remain intact. Our chicks need a lot of food now to grow, and we need to avoid confusion. So, we *must* keep this a secret until we have worked out a good solution."

Alice cleared her throat loudly, then spoke with a steely resolve. "When we have a problem, forming a committee and trying to protect our colony from unpleasant news is what we normally do. But this is *far, far* from a normal problem."

The others looked at her. The unasked question on everyone's mind was: *Where was she going with this line of reasoning?*

Alice said, "We must immediately call a general assembly of the colony and convince as many as possible that there is a big problem. We must get enough of our friends and families on our side so that we have a chance of finding a solution that many will accept."

Normally penguins behave in quite a controlled manner, especially if they are Leadership Council penguins sitting in a meeting. But now a few of the birds went completely wild, all talking at the same time.

"An assembly!!" "…the risk is…" "…never have we…" "… a panic…" "…no, no, no…" "…and what would we say?"

It was not a pretty sight.

"I have an idea," Fred said cautiously. "Would you give me a few minutes, please? I won't be long."

The others said nothing. Fred took that to be a yes—or at least not a no.

He moved as quickly as possible down the mountain, found what he wanted, and climbed back up. The Group of Ten birds were jabbering once again. They stopped when Fred arrived with a glass bottle.

"What's this?" asked Alice.

"I don't really know," Fred said. "My father found it one summer washed up to the edge of our iceberg. It looks like ice, but it is not made from ice." He pecked on the bottle with the tip of his beak. "It's much harder than ice and if you sit on it, it warms up but it doesn't melt."

Everyone stared. So…?

"Perhaps we could fill it with water, seal the hole on top, and place it in the cold wind. Then tomorrow we can see if it is broken by the force of the expanding water as it freezes."

Fred paused as the rest of the group worked their way through the logic of his statements.

He continued. "And if it doesn't break apart, then perhaps you should not rush ahead and call an assembly of the colony."

Alice was fascinated. Risky, she thought to herself, but is this bird clever or what?!

NoNo suspected it was a trick but saw no easy out. And maybe it would stop all the foolishness.

Louis, the Head Penguin, looked at NoNo.

Louis made his judgment. He told the others, "Then let it be done."

And they did.

Louis put water into the bottle. He sealed it with a fish bone that was just the right size. He gave the bottle to Buddy, a quiet and boyishly handsome penguin who everyone seemed to like and trust.

And then they dispersed.

Fred was always willing to stick his neck out if necessary, though it inevitably made him nervous. So he did not sleep particularly well that night.

The next morning when Buddy climbed up the hill, all the others were there looking down at him. When he reached the top, one of the birds said, "Well?"

Buddy produced the bottle. It was clearly broken from ice that had grown too big to fit inside.

"I'm convinced," Buddy told them.

The birds jabbered for half an hour. All except two said that they needed to act. One of the two, of course, was NoNo. "You may be onto something" he said, "but…"

He was more or less ignored.

Louis said, "Let the others know we will have an assembly. Do not tell them the topic yet."

The colony's birds were curious about the reason for the assembly. But Alice made sure the Leadership Council members kept their beaks shut—which built up a bit of interest and suspense.

Nearly all the adults showed up. Most of the talk was about normal life on their iceberg.

"Felix is getting fat. Too much fish, too little exercise."

"Where is he getting all the fish?"

"Ahh, now *that* is an interesting story."

Louis called the meeting to order and quickly turned it over to Alice.

Alice told of her swim with Fred, the many signs of melting, and the open cave filled with water. Fred showed his model of the iceberg and explained why he thought they were in danger. Buddy told the story of the glass bottle. And Louis, as Head Penguin, ended the session by saying that in his opinion they had to act, and though he was not sure how, he was confident they would find a solution.

By the time everyone had a chance to see the model and the bottle up close, to ask both Fred and Alice questions, and to hear more from Louis, the meeting had lasted most of the morning.

The birds were stunned, even those who normally responded to anything by saying "well yes, but…." The complacent sense that all is just fine-fine-fine-thank-you began to drain into the vast ocean. Fred, Louis, and Alice were certainly not aware of it—professional change experts they were not—but by reducing complacency and increasing urgency they had taken exactly the right first step in potentially saving the colony.

When the meeting broke up, the jabbering began.

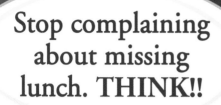

I Cannot Do the Job Alone

The next morning a friend of NoNo's slid up to Louis. Penguins can slide on their stomachs, though it looks bizarre to humans. He suggested that as the Head Penguin, it was Louis's DUTY to solve the melting iceberg problem by himself. "That's what leaders do. You are a great leader. You need no help." The bird then slid (one might say slithered) away. Another penguin suggested that Louis delegate the problem to the young birds who were the experts on ice. Louis pointed out, patiently, that those birds had no credibility in the colony, had no known leadership skills, were very inexperienced, and a few were not well liked. The bird making this suggestion said, "So what's your point?"

Louis thought about what next step he should take, then called Alice, Fred, Buddy, and a penguin named Jordan to a quiet spot on the northwest side of the iceberg. Jordan was known as the "Professor" since he was the closest the Leadership Council had to an intellectual. If a university were located on their iceberg, Jordan would have been a tenured member of the faculty.

The Head Penguin said, "The colony needs a *team* of birds to guide it through this difficult period. I cannot do the job alone. I believe the five of us are the best team for the task ahead."

Alice nodded ever so slightly. Buddy looked confused. Fred was surprised that he, a more junior penguin, was being included. But the Professor was the first to speak.

"Why do you make the assumption that the five of us can succeed?" he asked.

Louis nodded in his normal patient manner. Alice hid her irritation. If she had had a watch, which she didn't, she would have been looking at it while tapping her foot.

"It is a reasonable question," the Head Penguin said. "Look at the five of us, Professor. Define the challenge clearly. Make a list in your mind of each of our strengths. Deduce an answer to your own question."

Louis never talked this way, except when he was speaking to the Professor.

Jordan looked off toward the horizon. If you could have heard the thoughts flashing through his penguin brain, they would have been something like this:

- Louis. Head Penguin. Enough experience to be wise. Patient. A bit conservative. Not easily flustered. Respected by almost all except NoNo and the teenagers. Smart (but not an intellectual heavyweight).

- Alice. Practical. Aggressive. Makes things happen. Doesn't care about status and treats everyone the same. Impossible to intimidate, so don't even try. Smart (but not an intellectual heavyweight).

- Buddy. Boyishly handsome. Not the slightest bit ambitious. Well trusted and liked (maybe your wife likes him too much). *Definitely* not an intellectual heavyweight.

- Fred. Younger. Amazingly curious and creative. Level-headed. Nice beak. Insufficient data to judge his I.Q.

- Me. Logical (actually, very logical). Well read. Fascinated by interesting questions. Not the most social of birds, but then why would anyone want to be a social bird?

- Thus, if the Head Penguin is A, Alice is B, Buddy is C, Fred is D, and I am E, then A + B + C + D+ E clearly equals a strong group.

The Professor turned to Louis and said, "What you say is remarkably logical."

Buddy looked confused, as he often did. He never really understood the Professor, but he trusted Louis. Alice's irritation calmed a bit as she was once again reminded of why the Head Penguin was the Head Penguin.

Fred couldn't imagine what went on in the Professor's head. But like Alice and Louis, Fred sensed they were on the right track. He also felt privileged to be working with this talented group of senior birds.

They spent the rest of the day together. The conversation was difficult at first:

"I wonder by what percentage our home is shrinking each year," the Professor said at one point. "I once read that a bird named Vladiwitch created a method…"

Alice coughed twice. Loudly. While staring intensely at Louis, she said, "Maybe we should concentrate on what we are going to do tomorrow."

Buddy said softly, "I'm sure Mr. Vladiwitch was a very nice bird."

The Professor nodded, pleased that someone was joining his conversation, even if it was only Buddy.

Louis redirected the dialogue. "I think it would help if we all closed our eyes for a moment." Before the Professor could question the relevance of eye closing, the Head Penguin said, "Please don't ask why. Tolerate an old bird's suggestion. This will only require a minute."

The others, one after the other, closed their eyes.

Louis said, "With your eyes shut, point east."
After a moment of hesitation, all did so.
"Now open your eyes," he told them.

Buddy, the Professor, Fred, and Alice all pointed in different directions. Buddy even pointed slightly upward toward the sky.

Alice sighed, intuitively sensing the problem. The Professor said, "Ah, yes, fascinating." Fred nodded ever so slightly. Buddy was lost.

The Professor said, "You see, for us, A + B is additive—that is to say, more capable than two individuals by themselves—only if A and B can work as a team. Yet we responded to Louis's task as individuals. He did not say we couldn't work together, could not talk or touch each other. You see, Flotbottom's theory of group…"

The Head Penguin interrupted the speech by raising his wing, then saying "Would anyone like squid for lunch?" This stopped the overweight professor, whose grumbling stomach easily trumped his brain. Buddy said, "What a great idea."

Penguins LOVE squid, those sea creatures that come in sizes ranging from as large as a bus—like Jules Verne's monster in *20,000 Leagues Under the Sea*—to smaller than a mouse. But the tiny squid so liked by the penguins are tricky little devils. They will shoot a very unappealing jet of black ink at a predator and then zoom away. So in a one squid versus one penguin matchup, the squid can easily win. Penguins, having discovered this problem many, many years ago, had found a solution: hunt squid in groups.

Louis jumped into the sea first, quickly followed by the others. Although penguins wobble awkwardly back and forth on land—looking a bit like Charlie Chaplin—in the water they move with extraordinary skill and grace. They can dive a third of a mile beneath the surface, stay under water for up to twenty minutes, and maneuver better than a $250,000 Porsche. But…extraordinary individual capabilities do not a squid catch.

The first squid they encountered actually escaped. But soon the penguins learned to work together well—coordinating their movements, surrounding the lunch. Eventually, enough food for everyone was found, even for the Professor's rather large appetite.

After a satisfying meal, Louis led a discussion that rarely touched on the melting iceberg or what the five of them needed to do next. Instead he focused on life, loved ones, and their hopes and dreams. They talked for hours.

The Professor was disinclined to just talk about life without structure around the conversation to give it some RIGOR. So he kept his beak shut and let his analytical brain work quietly. Melting iceberg. Fred finds it. Tough sell to a complacent group. Goes to Alice first. Shows her the problem. The ice model. The bottle. The group meeting. Complacency reduced. Louis picks group to guide the effort. Interesting makeup. Turning nonteam into team with squid and talk.

All rather strange, but fascinating.

The next morning, Louis kept them together. He would have liked a month to turn the five birds into a close-knit team. But he did not have a month. So he did the best he could, and within two days the penguins certainly looked much less like individuals pointing in different directions. Louis had largely succeeded in taking the difficult but essential step of <u>pulling together a team to guide the needed change.</u>

The Seagull

An impatient Alice suggested they search rapidly for solutions to their melting-iceberg problem by talking to others in the colony. The Head Penguin was not sure that talking to others was the best next step, and the Professor definitely did not see the point. But after a constructive discussion, Alice prevailed.

One bird—who had the heart of a Texas oilman— suggested they drill a hole from the surface down to the cave to let out water and pressure. This would not solve the more general problem of the melting, but it might keep their home from exploding during the upcoming winter. This drill-a-hole idea was briefly discussed before the Professor pointed out that with all 268 birds pecking away 24 hours a day, they would break through to the cave in 5.2 years.

Next.

Another bird suggested they find a perfect iceberg. No melting, no exposed caves, no fissures, just wonderful in every way so that their children and grandchildren would never, ever have to face a crisis like this again. Perhaps if they appointed a perfect-iceberg committee? Fortunately, Alice was not around to hear this.

Another idea: somehow move the colony toward the center of Antarctica where the ice is thicker and stronger. Although none of the penguins had any idea of the size of the continent—more than one and a half times the size of the United States!—one very heavyset bird said, "Won't that take us a long way from water? How will I get fish?"

Next.

One penguin on the Leadership Council suggested creating a sort of superglue out of killer-whale blubber and using it to glue the iceberg together "real tight." He admitted that this would not solve the more general problem of melting, but it might avert immediate disaster.

They were obviously getting desperate.

Then an older and highly respected member of the colony suggested that they try something new. "Maybe you should do what Fred did when he found our terrible problem. Walk around, keeping your eyes and minds open. Be curious." The Head Penguin, recognizing the need for a different approach, agreed. "Let's try it," he said, and so they did.

They went west. They saw beautiful walls of snow. They saw families doing things families do. They overheard conversations about melting and fish. They listened to birds who needed to share their anxieties.

Then after an hour or so, Fred, in his typically respectful way, said: "Up there."

Fred was looking at a seagull. Since normally there are no seagulls in Antarctica, they all stared. A small, white, flying penguin? Probably not.

"Fascinating," said the Professor. "I have a theory about animals that fly. You see—" Before he could continue, Alice tapped him on his shoulder. He had learned in the prior two days that Alice tapping him like that meant "you're wonderful, Professor, but please shut up," which he did.

"What is it?" asked Buddy.

"I don't know," Fred said, "but a bird can't fly forever. It must have a home on the ground. But it's so cold here."

They agreed. If the seagull tried to live with them, it would freeze as hard as a rock in less than a week.

Fred continued, "I suppose it could be very, very lost, but it does not seem to be afraid. What if moving from one piece of land to another was just the way it lived? What if it's a…"

Fred used the closest word penguins have for *nomad.*

Alice said, "You aren't suggesting…?"

The Head Penguin said, "I wonder."

The Professor said, "Fascinating."

Buddy said, "I'm sorry, but what are you talking about?"

The Head Penguin responded to Buddy by saying, simply, "We are thinking about the possibility of a new and very different way of life."

They talked for hours and hours. If we… But then… How would we…? No, you see… Yes, but we could… Why not…? Just maybe…

Buddy asked, "So what do we do next?"

The Head Penguin said, "We need to think this through carefully."

Alice said, "We need to move fast."

The Professor said, "But quality of thought is more important than speed."

Alice continued, "First we need to learn more about that flying bird, and now."

The Head Penguin agreed. The Professor went looking for something to write on. Then they all went to search for the seagull.

Fred had in him a bit of Sherlock Holmes, the famous nonpenguin detective. So within a half hour, they found the seagull.

Alice whispered to Buddy, "Say 'hello' to the bird."

In the warm and gentle voice that came naturally, Buddy said, "Hi. This is Alice." He pointed at her. "That's Louis, Fred, and the Professor. I'm Buddy."

The seagull just stared at them.

"Where do you come from?" Buddy asked. "And what are you looking for here?"

The seagull kept its distance, but did not fly away. Finally he said, "I'm a scout. I fly ahead of the clan looking for where we might live next."

The Professor began to ask questions—useful questions, though he did go off on tangents occasionally (always brought back by You-Know-Who).

In response, the seagull told the penguins of his clan's nomadic existence. He talked about what they ate (which, frankly, sounded to the penguins like just about anything). He spoke of what it was like to be a scout. When he began to turn blue and have trouble speaking, he said good-bye and flew away.

The Professor and Buddy were not totally convinced that what was appropriate for seagulls could possibly be right for penguins. "We're different." "They fly." "We eat delicious fresh fish." "They seem to eat, well…yuck."

"Of course we're different," Alice said with considerably more diplomacy than usual. "That means we can't just copy them. But the idea is very interesting.

I can almost see how we might live. We'd learn to move around. We wouldn't stay in one place forever. We wouldn't try to fix melting icebergs. We would just face up to the fact that what sustains us cannot go on forever."

The Professor asked dozens of questions. Louis said little but thought a great deal about the discussion and its implications.

Alice said, "I wonder why someone didn't think of this idea as soon as we realized that our iceberg was melting?"

The Professor said, "Surely *someone* in the colony did. It is so...logical."

The Professor turned his head to the right. What he saw was:

Well, the Professor thought, maybe not.

The Head Penguin said, "After living one way for so long, why should it be easy to think of a whole new way of life?"

The Professor realized that no one had offered a solid theory about why their home was melting. He had been assuming that melting and degradation must have occurred slowly over a long period of time. But what if that weren't true?

What if something had caused the problem suddenly? But what could that possibly be? Should he have urged his fellow penguins to take more time and be more systematic in thinking about their iceberg problem? But there was so little time.

Unanswered questions disturbed the Professor greatly. But that evening, he slept remarkably well under the circumstances. He believed the team had succeeded in <u>creating a vision</u> of a new future, and one that seemed plausible. He was beginning to see how they could create that future. He was (oddly) comforted that Louis, Alice, Fred, and Buddy were thinking the same way.

Getting the Message Out

The following day, Louis called for a meeting at noon of the entire colony. As you would expect at this point, nearly everyone showed up—so there would be again no lunch for the increasingly desperate leopard seals.

An energized Professor spent the entire morning preparing a sort of 97-slide PowerPoint presentation for Louis to use in communicating their vision. The Head Penguin looked over the material, which was very impressive, then gave it to Buddy. After studying the Professor's work, Buddy said, "I'm sorry, but I'm a little lost." Louis asked where he had become stuck. Buddy told him it was on slide #2. Alice shut her eyes and did deep breathing exercises.

The Head Penguin looked again at the presentation created by the Professor. It was, in its way, beautifully done. But Louis kept thinking about how difficult it would be to help the colony understand his message. How do you talk to birds who were anxious, preoccupied, skeptical, tradition bound, or unimaginative?

Louis decided he needed to try a different method, even though it could be risky. He did not like risk, but…

Louis began the colony's assembly by saying, "Fellow penguins, as we meet this challenge—*and we definitely will*—it is more important than ever to remember *who we really are*."

The crowd looked blankly at him.

"Tell me, are we penguins who deeply respect one another?"

There was silence until someone said, "Of course." Then others said, "Yes."

NoNo was in the middle of the audience trying to figure out what scheme was afoot. It was not obvious yet, which he did not like.

Louis continued. "And do we strongly value discipline?" "Yes," said a dozen or so of the elderly birds.

"And do we have a strong sense of responsibility, too?" It was hard to argue with that. It had been true for generations. "Yes," many now agreed.

"Above all, do we stand for brotherhood and the love of our young?" A loud "Yes!" followed.

The Head Penguin paused. "And tell me…are these beliefs and shared values linked to *a large piece of ice?*"

When some not particularly bright birds, caught up in the yes-yes cadence, were again about to say "Yes," Alice shouted "NO!" She was quickly followed by the Professor, Fred, and few of the younger birds. Then many penguins muttered a "No, no, no" to themselves.

"No," Louis agreed.

The birds stood still, all looking at the Head Penguin. Some didn't know that he could speak so forcefully—and so emotionally.

"I'd like you now to listen to Buddy," Louis said after another dramatic pause. "He will tell you a story that inspired us to think of a new and better way of life."

So Buddy started to tell the seagull's story: "He is a scout for his clan. He explores the territory to find good places for his colony to move next. *Imagine, they are free! They go wherever they like to go.* You see, many, many years ago, they…"

Buddy told what he knew of the history of the seagull clan, of the way they lived now, and of the bird he had met. Buddy wasn't aware of it, but he was a very good storyteller.

When he was done, the penguins had many questions. Some of the slower birds struggled with the idea of a flying animal. Some just wanted to know every detail of what the seagull had said. There were many side discussions, especially about "freedom" and a nomadic existence. The faster birds were quick to see the vision without it ever being stated explicitly.

Louis let the jabbering go on for a while. Then he cleared his throat loudly and asked for order. When the noise subsided, he told the crowd, with conviction, "This iceberg is not who we *are*. It is only where we now *live*. We are smarter, stronger, and more capable than the seagulls. So why can't we do what they have done, and better? We are not chained to this piece of ice. We can leave it behind us. Let it melt to the size of a fish. Let it break into one thousand pieces. We will find other places to live that are safer. When necessary, we will move again. We will never have to put our families at risk from the sort of terrible danger we face today. WE WILL PREVAIL!"

NoNo's blood pressure hit 240 over 160.

By the end of the meeting, if you could have carefully studied the eyes of the crowd, you would probably have concluded that:

- 30 percent of the colony could see a new way of living, were convinced the vision had merit, and were relieved;

- 30 percent were digesting what they had heard and seen;

- 20 percent were very confused;

- 10 percent were skeptical but not hostile; and

- 10 percent were like NoNo, convinced this was all completely absurd.

The Head Penguin thought to himself, "good enough for now," and so he ended the meeting.

Alice grabbed Fred, Buddy, and the Professor, and said, "Follow me." Being sensible birds, they did so.

She quickly explained her latest idea: to come up with slogans to be put on iceposters. "We need to remind the birds of what they have heard, and remind them ALL THE TIME. The meeting this morning was brief. Some of the colony were not here. The message is radical. We need much more communication—everyday, everywhere."

Buddy wondered, aloud, "Will so many posters be annoying to some of our friends?" Alice replied, "Given a choice between a few annoyed birds and a melting, exploding iceberg with screaming penguins on it, I'd choose annoyed." Put that way...

They began creating posters. At first they struggled.

But with the help of some of the more creative birds—some of whom were younger than Fred— they quickly got the hang of it.

Every day for a week, twenty penguins came up with new slogans and put them on iceposters scattered around the iceberg. When the birds could find no more places for the posters, Alice suggested they put them underwater next to the most popular and productive fishing grounds. Sounds a little odd, but (1) penguins can see very clearly underwater, (2) there were no posters there, yet, (3) when penguins look for fish, they cannot close their eyes, even if they are annoyed.

The dramatic meeting, Louis's "we are not an iceberg" speech, Buddy's storytelling about the seagull, and Alice's countless iceposters began to have the desired effect. Many birds, though far from all, came to see and accept what they had to do.

Communicating the new vision of a nomadic life, of a very different future, was for the most part remarkably successful.

The colony had taken yet another big step forward. You could tell just by watching the birds.

Good News, Bad News

Thirty to forty birds began to work in small groups to plan for the selection of scouts, the mapping of trips to find new icebergs, and the logistics of moving the colony. Louis was cautiously optimistic.

Over the next week, there was both good news and bad.

Good: Although some birds were still anxious, enthusiasm among the core group of planners began to grow and grow.

Mostly Good: Nearly a dozen birds expressed interest in being scouts—the job of looking for a new home for the colony. Unfortunately, the group was mostly made up of adolescents who showed less concern for finding a new iceberg than for putting more excitement into lives that lacked video games and Nikes.

Not so good: NoNo and a few of his friends seemed to be everywhere forecasting storms and dangerous currents. Many penguins ignored them, but far from all.

Mysterious: A few of the very young penguins started having scary dreams. When Alice looked into the problem, she found that the kindergarten teacher had developed an affinity for telling the children horror stories about ghastly killer whales hunting young penguins. The nightmares caused much uproar among the parents, including some who were possible candidates to become scouts. Why was the good-natured teacher creating this problem?

Not mysterious at all, but certainly not helpful: Some members of the Leadership Council thought the scouts would need a boss. When they began to lobby for the role of President of the Scouts, irritating conflict among the Council members grew.

And finally, there was…

Very troubling news: Penguins need a lot of food to build up fat for the winter. Someone pointed out that the difficult task of exploring the vast territory around the iceberg would leave the scouts with insufficient time to fish. This problem was made much worse because of a long-standing tradition in the colony that birds shared their food with their children, and ONLY with their children. No adults caught fish for other adults. It simply was not done.

The effect of the good news at first outweighed the bad. But then NoNo's antics, anxious children, anxiety among the parents of anxious children, infighting in the Leadership Council, and the feeding-the-scouts problem began to take their toll.

NoNo and a few of his friends saw the obstacles and were encouraged. Maybe if they worked a little harder . . .

Amanda was one of the most enthusiastic and hardworking of the birds in the group of planners. She believed in the vision of a new way of life. She worked fourteen-hour days to help make it a reality. But then her husband, unnerved by NoNo's pronouncements, demanded that she stop. Long, difficult conversations ensued. Then her child's nightmares became so chilling that she found herself spending half the night tending to the little bird. When she heard about the feeding-the-scouts problem, her level of frustration outgrew her initial excitement. Feeling powerless to deal with forces beyond her control, she started to skip the planning meetings.

And she was not alone.

By Thursday that week, three other birds were also missing the meetings. By Friday, that number had grown to eight; by Saturday, to fifteen.

The bird chairing those planning meetings tried to stop the outflow of membership with a clear restatement of the facts. *Iceberg melting. Must change. Have a good vision. Time for implementation.* The logic was impeccable. And it had no effect on the dropping attendance.

Alice saw that many of the more enthusiastic birds were becoming very frustrated by the mounting obstacles. "We have to deal with this," she told Louis, "and quickly." He agreed.

Buddy, Fred, the Professor, Louis, and Alice discussed the situation, identified what needed to be done, and agreed upon what role each of them would play. Such quick agreement was not necessarily a sign of panic, but close to it.

Even as they met, NoNo was everywhere.

"The gods are very mad," he told crowd after crowd. "They will send a gigantic killer whale to eat all our fish. Its enormous mouth will bite our iceberg into pieces and crush our children in its awful jaws. It will create five hundred-foot waves. We must stop this nonsense about 'nomads' *immediately*."

Louis pulled NoNo aside and told him (truthfully) that weather forecasting would be more important in the future and that they needed to add more science to their approach.

NoNo listened, warily.

"Therefore," Louis said, "I have asked the Professor to help us."

NoNo angrily turned around to leave and found the Professor was already beside him.

"Did you read the article by Himlish on iceberg trauma?" the Professor asked. "I believe it was published in the late 1960s." NoNo ran. The Professor followed.

And *everywhere* that NoNo went…

In a very direct way, Louis also dealt with those lobbying to be President of the Scouts.

It was a short, very firm discussion. "Enough!" he told them.

Buddy's major role in the plan was to talk to the kindergarten teacher. The misty-eyed bird shared her fears with the Penguin Everyone Liked—fears that clearly had been influencing her choice of the stories she was reading to the children.

"With all the change," she told him, nearly sobbing, "the colony may not need a kindergarten. It, it…may not need a teacher who is a bit too old to adapt."

She was very upset. Buddy was very sympathetic. When she stopped speaking, he told her: "No. The little birds will need to learn even *more* in a world that will be ever changing. A kindergarten will be *more* important."

Her sobbing slowed. Buddy continued to speak of the essential role of schooling after all the changes.

"I am very confident," he concluded, with complete sincerity, "that you can help them learn what is needed. You are a wonderful teacher. If you need to make adjustments here and there, I know you'll do it because you care so much for the little penguins."

He was reassuring. He was patient. He calmly and sincerely repeated his message again and again. She felt so relieved and happy that she wanted to kiss him.

It was a truly touching scene.

The actions by Louis, the Professor, and Buddy—with still others by Fred and Alice—all had an immediate effect.

NoNo created no new mischief (though he certainly wanted to). No matter where he went, the Professor was right beside him, talking and talking and talking.

"A regression of six variables has shown…"

"If you don't stop following me," NoNo screamed, "I'm going to…"

"Yes, yes. Now pay particular attention to this point. The regression…"

"Aaaggggh…"

After her chat with Buddy, the kindergarten teacher gathered her young students together to tell them tales of heroic action to help others under difficult and changing circumstances. She found some great stories. She told them with enthusiasm.

She explained that the colony would be needing heroes to deal with new challenges, and that anyone, including the youngest of them, could help. The students loved it.

That same evening, most of the nightmares stopped.

The number of penguins actively working in the core group had dropped from thirty-five to eighteen. But now, as obstacles to change were being removed, as fewer and fewer of the more enthusiastic birds were feeling frustrated, distracted, or powerless, the numbers began to rise again.

Louis calculated that they would need around fifty birds to do all the work that had to be completed quickly. He didn't have fifty yet, but at least the trend was in the right direction.

Sally Ann was just a kindergarten student. Her mind was filled with all the new stories of heroic action. While waddling home from school, she saw Alice. As youngsters do when they don't know any better, she approached this important bird and said, "Excuse me. How can I become a hero?" Alice stopped and looked at her. Preoccupied with the melting, the general mood of the colony, and the feeding-the-scouts problem, she barely heard the question. The youngster repeated it. Instead of saying, "Just go home to your mother," Alice told her, "If you could make your parents understand that the Head Penguin needs their help, especially in catching fish to feed the scouts, then you would be a true hero."

"That's all?" the little one replied, with all the hopeful naïveté of the young.

The next day, the child talked to her friends, and she had many friends. And from those discussions, an idea was born of how the children could help the colony make a nomadic life a reality. The kindergarten teacher canceled a few regular classes—broke a few rules—and helped give the idea some structure. It came to be called "Tribute to Our Heroes Day."

Some parents were nervous about all this activity. <u>Making everyone</u>, even the children, <u>feel empowered</u> was unprecendented in the colony. But the chicks loved it.

The Scouts

Louis decided they would need evidence, and quickly, that their efforts were on the right track. So his next step was to ask Fred to select a small, elite group of athletic and highly motivated scouts, coordinate their schedules, and send them off to search for potential new homes.

"The colony needs to see progress as soon as possible," the Head Penguin told Fred. "And we must do everything conceivable to help the scouts devise the means to protect themselves. We need every one of those birds to return safely and as fast as possible. Even one missing bird will create more anxiety and make NoNo's warnings more credible. Remember, they don't need to pick a new home, just find us a few possibilities."

The scouts were organized and left the next day. Fred had chosen well. They were strong, bright, and highly enthusiastic.

The toughest single challenge facing the colony was gathering enough fresh fish to feed the tired and hungry scouts when they returned to their home. They would each need a huge meal of fish immediately—up to twenty pounds worth which, incredibly, a penguin can easily eat at one sitting.

But…there was that very old tradition in the colony in which birds (1) shared their food with their children, (2) shared their food ONLY with their children.

So who would catch fish for the scouts?

Into the void of practical solutions came little Sally Ann, the kindergartner, with her "Tribute to Our Heroes Day" idea.

The Heroes Day Celebration would include a raffle, performances, a band, and a flea market. The unusual price of admission: two fish per adult.

The young birds explained the festive day to their parents. As you might imagine, some preoccupied adults could not quite grasp what they were hearing, some did not like the idea much at all, and some were not even aware that scouts had left the iceberg. Yet many were proud of their children for being creative in a time of need.

Still, parents felt a bit awkward. "You don't share food, except with your children" was a very, very old and established tradition. So the inspired youngsters made it clear that they would be *extremely* embarrassed unless (1) their parents came to Heroes Day, and (2) each mother and father brought two fish as the cost of admission.

As soon as a few parents relented, announcing that they would be bringing fish, others decided they must also. Social pressure works as well in penguin colonies as in human colonies.

Louis scheduled Heroes Day to coincide with the time the scouts were scheduled to return. From early in the morning until late in the afternoon, the event was an astonishing success. The games, band, raffle, and other events were great fun for everyone. But the climax came at the end, as the birds waited for the scouts.

NoNo predicted half would never make it back. "Whale food," he told as many as would listen to him. "The fools will get lost." Some birds nodded their heads, so he kept saying it. NoNo was relentless. He worked harder that day than he had in years.

Some in the colony were nervous, quite apart from NoNo's antics. Some were still skeptical about the claims being made. All of which made the end of the day even more dramatic.

Every single scout returned, one after the other, although a few looked like they were at death's door, and one was seriously hurt. Alice was waiting with a well-organized crew to care for any injury. Which they did.

Almost as soon as the scouts arrived, they began to tell amazing tales about the sea, about swimming long distances, and about new icebergs they had seen. Everyone crowded around the birds.

Because they were so hungry, the scouts quickly and happily ate the fish that the other penguins had brought to the fair. Even as they were stuffing themselves, you could see that most of Fred's volunteers were extremely excited about what they had done. When they were finished, Sally Ann and her little friends gave the scouts ribbons to go around their necks. Made by the children, the ribbons were all tied to glittering ice medals with the simple inscription, HERO.

The crowd cheered. The scouts beamed (or at least as much as a penguin can beam).

Louis called for the child who had put in motion the events leading to the festive day. In front of the colony, he said, "And this is for our youngest hero." He handed Sally Ann the broken bottle which had become somewhat legendary since first shown to all the birds. The crowd applauded enthusiastically.

The child cried small tears of joy. Her parents were puffed up with pride. Alice was as happy as she could remember being in years.

Discussions went late into the night, well after the children had been put to bed. Many in the colony continued to be amazed at what the scouts told them, even when it was said a second or third time. Most of the birds who were skeptical of a nomadic life found themselves becoming less skeptical. Birds who were enthusiastic felt more enthusiastic. Again, under trying circumstances, the colony had taken a very important step forward.

Fred and the Scouts had succeeded in <u>creating</u> (what one MBA-sounding bird called) "<u>a short-term win.</u>" It was a big win.

NoNo was nowhere in sight. He seemed to have been magically replaced by scouts wearing ribbons attached to medals.

The Second Wave

The next morning, Louis called a meeting of the scouts. The Professor was also invited.

"What did you learn?" the Head Penguin asked the birds. "What icebergs did you see that might be big enough, in good shape, able to protect our eggs during the winter, and close enough so that our children and elderly can safely travel there?"

The scouts discussed what they had found. The Professor asked question after question after question to distinguish opinions from facts. His style did not make him popular with all the birds—he could not have cared less—but it was very effective.

After the Heroes Day, more birds volunteered to be among the second wave of scouts, even though their task of selecting a single iceberg might be very taxing. Louis chose a team from among the volunteers and sent them off to explore promising possibilities discovered by the first wave of scouts.

Many of the skeptics in the colony were now becoming much less skeptical. Some birds still had reservations, many of which were rational. A few of the penguins were just nervous by nature.

Almost no one was paying any attention to NoNo anymore.

Alice was relentless in keeping up the momentum of the work. Some on the Leadership Council complained that they did not have time to deal with all the issues that were arising. Alice pointed out that half their traditional Leadership Council meetings were irrelevant. "Eliminate them," she said bluntly. Louis did.

At one point, even the Head Penguin suggested that the right step might be to slow down. But Alice wouldn't hear of it.

"We are constantly at risk of losing our courage. Some birds are already suggesting we wait until next winter. Then, if we are still alive, they will say the danger was overstated and that any change is not needed."

It was a good point.

The second wave of scouts found an iceberg that looked suitable for a number of reasons. It was:

- A safe home. No evidence of melting or water filled caves.

- Equipped with a tall snowwall to protect them from the icy storms.

- Close to good fishing sites.

- Located on a route with enough small icebergs or ice plateaus along the way to give the youngest and oldest penguins some rest during the journey.

The returning scouts were proud, excited, and very happy. The rest of the colony was proud, excited and happy to see them.

By this time, the chore of gathering fish for scouts was already beginning to seem like a part of the normal routine. Many birds helped. It was all rather astonishing.

The Professor was asked to assess more scientifically the newly found piece of ice and snow. He was not enthusiastic about this task. He was overweight and the journey to the new iceberg was not a short one. But after a quiet chat with Louis (and a not so quiet chat with Alice), he announced he was ready to accompany a group of scouts. And he did.

Meanwhile the colony was busy with other important, though pleasant, routines, like creating new little penguins.

Then on May the 12th, just before the start of Antarctica's winter, the birds began their move to their new home. It was not a moment too soon.

The move was chaotic at times. At one point, a few penguins were lost and there was a panic. But those birds found their way back to the others, and for the most part, all went as well as one could hope.

Because of his effective leadership, Louis became greatly admired by the colony. Yet, to his credit, he did not allow his pride to slide into arrogance.

Buddy soothed the worried, encouraged the down-trodden, calmed the frantic, and probably had another ten female birds fall in love with him (but that's another story).

When no one could think of a solution to a new problem, Fred was called in to display his level-headed creativity.

The Professor loved his new status in the colony. He even found, oddly, that he enjoyed the admiration of birds he thought had no brains at all.

Alice seemed to exist on three hours of sleep a day.

And NoNo predicted doom until the very end.

The winter passed. The colony had problems. Their new home was different, the best fishing grounds were in unfamiliar places, the winds bounced off walls of ice in unexpected ways. But the problems were not as large as the anxious birds had feared.

The next season, the scouts found a still better iceberg, larger and with richer fishing grounds. And though it was tempting to declare that the colony had been subjected to enough change, and should stay forever on their new home, they didn't. They moved again. It was a critical step: not becoming complacent again and not letting up.

As you might imagine, the preparation for the second move was less traumatic than the first.

The Most Remarkable Change

You might reasonably think our story is over. But it isn't quite.

Some birds began to talk about how they had now found the perfect iceberg and therefore…

Tradition dies a hard death. Culture changes with as much difficulty in penguin colonies as in human colonies.

Alice convinced Louis to shake up the Leadership Council. He was reluctant to do anything that would show disrespect for birds who had worked hard for years to help and serve the colony. Making the moves while preserving the dignity of all was not easy. But Alice was insistent, and when Alice was insistent, well, you know.

A tough selection process was created for scouts. They were also given more fish. And their status within the colony went up even further.

The penguin school system added "Scouting" as a new required subject in the curriculum.

The Professor took over as chief weather forecaster. A bit reluctant at first, he poured "real science" into the work and came to love the job.

Fred was asked to serve on the Leadership Council as Head of the Scouts. He was honored and accepted.

Buddy was offered a number of more important jobs. He turned them all down, but helped the Leadership Council find other good candidates. His lack of ambition came to be seen as great humility. The birds loved him even more.

Today, the colony moves around like nomads. Most have accepted it. Some love it. Some never will.

Louis retired, became the grandfather figure for the whole colony, and enjoyed his free time more than he expected. A now slightly more balanced Alice took his place as Head Penguin.

As time went on, the colony thrived. It grew and grew. It became more skilled at handling new dangers, at least in part from what it had learned from the melting adventure.

Grandfather Louis became the colony's number-one teacher. He was asked again and again by the younger birds to tell them the story of The Great Change. At first he was reluctant, fearing that he would sound like an old timer boasting about past successes—real or imagined. But eventually, he saw the importance of telling the chicks—in as interesting and fun a way as he could—about the specific steps the colony had taken.

He talked about Fred's finding that the iceberg was melting, then how they 1) created a sense of urgency in the colony to deal with a diffcult problem, 2) put a carefully selected group in charge of guiding the change, 3) found the sensible vision of a better future, 4) communicated that vision so others would understand and accept it, 5) removed as many obstacles to action as was practical, 6) created some sort of success quickly, 7) never let up until the new way of life was firmly established, and, 8) finally, <u>ensured that the changes would not be overcome by stubborn, hard-to-die traditions.</u>

Although Louis never said so explicitly in his telling of the story, he felt the most remarkable change of all was in how so many members of the colony had grown less afraid of change, were learning the specific steps needed to make any large adjustment to new circumstances, and worked well together to keep leaping into a better and better future.

The Former-Head-Penguin was particularly amazed at what even the youngsters were doing to help the colony. And for that, he loved them all the more.

The End
(of the story, not the book)

Changing and Succeeding

Fables can be fun, but their power, as with the penguin story, lies in helping you act smarter: producing more, achievement, less confusion, lower stress, and a general sense of being in control through understanding what is going on around you.

Some people have minds that process our penguin tale automatically, finding clever methods used by the birds, thinking about their own personal experiences in light of those methods, and seeing their options for a better future. But anyone, including those people, can benefit from more conscious thought, discussion, and guidance.

People from software engineers to executives, homemakers to pastors, high school students to retirees have consciously used the Penguin story to better achieve what they want and what their organizations need. The process is one you can adapt to your own circumstances.

First, **read and reflect** on the story. You might find it useful to read it more than once. You would be surprised how much is packed into our short tale.

Ask yourself questions that are suggested directly by the story: Am I living on a melting iceberg or an iceberg that could melt? Melting icebergs come in dozens of forms: product lines that are aging, schools that are becoming irrelevant, services that are decreasing in quality, a business strategy that makes increasingly little sense, a new strategy whose implementation is sinking into the ocean. Who are the NoNos around me? Who are the Alices and Freds? Who am I?

This reflection can be aided greatly by knowledge of Kotter's research on successful change, a brief summary of which is on the next three pages. You can examine, for each of the Eight Steps, how our clever penguins achieved what they achieved. Then you can look, step by step, at what you and your organization have been doing or are planning to do.

The Eight Step Process of Successful Change

Set the Stage

1. Create a Sense of Urgency.

   Help others see the need for change and the importance of acting immediately.

2. Pull Together the Guiding Team.

   Make sure there is a powerful group guiding the change—one with leadership skills, credibility, communications ability, authority, analytical skills, and a sense of urgency.

Decide What to Do

3. Develop the Change Vision and Strategy.

   Clarify how the future will be different from the past, and how you can make that future a reality.

Make it Happen

4. Communicate for Understanding and Buy In.

   Make sure as many others as possible understand and accept the vision and the strategy.

5. Empower Others to Act.

   Remove as many barriers as possible so that those who want to make the vision a reality can do so.

6. Produce Short-Term Wins.

   Create some visible, unambiguous successes as soon as possible.

7. Don't Let Up.

   Press harder and faster after the first successes. Be relentless with initiating change after change until the vision is a reality.

Make It Stick

8. Create a New Culture.

   Hold on to the new ways of behaving, and make sure they succeed, until they become strong enough to replace old traditions.

The Role of Thinking and Feeling

Thinking differently can help change behavior and lead to better results.

- Collect data, analyze it.

- Present the information logically to change people's thinking.

- Changed thinking, in turn, can change behavior.

Feeling differently can change behavior MORE and lead to even better results.

- Create surprising, compelling, and, if possible, visual experiences.

- The experiences change how people feel about a situation.

- A change in feelings can lead to a significant change in behavior.

If you are an analytical person, a formal analysis in four columns—the eight steps, what the birds did, what you and your groups have been doing, what you might do—can be a powerful method of reflection.

After reading and reflecting, you **discuss the story with others** who have also read the book. The discussions can be informal, in training programs, as a part of regular on-the-job meetings, or with friends and family.

Penguin language (icebergs, Alice, hero medals) can both facilitate commnication and make discussions of difficult topics less confusing and threatening. Experience has taught us that these sorts of discussions can be very helpful.

You **find other tools** to help apply the lessons in the fable. For anyone who likes research-based business books, *Leading Change* and *Heart of Change* can be very useful. More information on each is found on page 135.

Today we have high-tech tools. We will be posting stories about what people have actually done as a result of the penguin fable, methods for facilitating a dialogue among people who have read the book, and more structured training exercises at www.ouricebergismelting.com.

With the tools, the discussions, and the book, you **find new and better ways to act** or find increased conviction to stay the course you are already on. You find ways to initiate change needed by an organization or group. You find ways to help with the initiatives of others. You apply the Eight Step method. In any case, you achieve more, gain more pride, have more fun, suffer fewer of the seemingly endless problems that can be created by a changing world, make your organization more successful, and put everyone less at risk.

Finally—and this can be the biggest payoff of the exercise—when you **act in concert with others,** because you have all read, reflected, and discussed the same fable, the end results can be very powerful.

Additional Resources: Books

The #1 management book of the year.

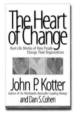
Real stories of people producing real change.

Additional Resources: Web Sites

www.ouricebergismelting.com
Tools for making change happen. Stories from people who have used *Our Iceberg Is Melting.*

www.theheartofchange.com
Information on *The Heart of Change,* including a diagnostic questionnaire.

www.johnkotter.com
Information about Dr. Kotter and his other books.

If we have learned one overwhelmingly important lesson in the past few years, it is this. When Leadership Council birds, the middle management penguiuns, and the chicks are all on the same page with regards to change, it is amazing what can happen, despite adverse conditions.

You can use this approach outside the workplace too—in community groups, sports teams, houses of worship, even in families. Once you start to think about it, you find there are melting icebergs, or icebergs vulnerable to melting, all over the place.

Listening to others, we never cease to be amazed at how many iceberg problems exist in our rapidly changing world. We never cease to be amazed at how difficult those problems can be to see and solve. But most of all, we never cease to be amazed at the creative ways people invent to jump ahead and develop better futures for very small groups, for very large organizations, and for themselves personally.

Humans can (sometimes) be even more clever than penguins.

The End
(except for readers wanting extra credit)

The Case for the Book

In 1996, John Kotter wrote *Leading Change.* It was named the #1 management book of the year by Executive General and has subsequently become the #1 bestselling book in the past decade on the subject of change within organizations. As much as we can tell, the framework in the book is used by more leaders more often than any other single methodology for dealing with large changes, no matter the form: creating more growth, eliminating inefficiencies, improving the quality of products or services, or redoing who does what and how.

Leading Change was based on extensive research that identified and defined the eight step pattern associated with highly successful change efforts. *Leading Change* talks about each of the steps in some depth.

Six years later Kotter wrote, with Dan Cohen, a follow-up book, *The Heart of Change*. It was also a bestseller and award winner. *The Heart of Change* was again based on extensive research that reconfirmed the findings from the original study and added an important new insight: People are less likely to change themselves and others based on data and analysis than on compelling experiences. Feelings often trump thinking. *The Heart of Change* explores this insight with more than twenty real stories from well-known businesses and various branches of the government.

During this period, Kotter became absolutely convinced that the rate of change was only going to continue to go up. He also became convinced that 90 percent of organizations were either ignoring relevant changes or were trying to adjust in ways that were not meeting their aspirations. Too much time and money was being spent to achieve too little, with too much pain and frustration all around.

Kotter also concluded that dealing with change was becoming an increasingly important skill for people not only at the top of organizations, but up and down hierarchies. In the most successful-change efforts Kotter researched, nearly everyone played crucial roles in helping enterprises adapt to a changing world. Yet in the vast majority of the organizations he studied, most people didn't know what to do, felt threatened, or were convinced top management didn't want their help. This inevitably led to wasted effort, poorer decisions, slower movement, and more frustration.

Enter Rathgeber. He was inspired by Kotter's award-winning books to develop a short training exercise about a penguin colony (the cover of *Leading Change* has a picture of penguins). The exercise was designed for use by senior and junior personnel. Kotter began collaborating with Rathgeber on that project, then suggested they write a book.

The resulting penguins fable drew on the frameworks in *Leading Change* and *The Heart of Change,* on additional lessons the authors have learned in the past few years about effective change, on a theory of learning through memorable stories and visual stimuli (like illustrations), and from current knowledge in neurology and related disciplines about how the human mind works. The end result does not look remotely like a typical professional book. It is a book that can seem at first glance either silly or dumbed down, but in fact is far from either.

Our goal in writing *Our Iceberg Is Melting* was to draw on the incredible power of good stories to influence behavior over time—making individuals and their groups more competent in handling change and producing better results. One of the beauties of a good story is that they can induce action from a broad range of people, in a manner quite different from most traditional professional books. The authors strongly believe that the world needs much more action from a broader range of people—action that is informed, committed, and inspired to help us all in an era of increasing change.

As of the time of this printing, we have run a dozen experiments with the book. Some have focused on individuals reading the manuscript, some on the use of the book in formal training, some on managers discussing the manuscript with their work groups, and some on simply giving books to large numbers of people in a company, a division of an organization, or a department. The goal of the latter has been to have a systems-wide effect—getting all the atoms vibrating on the same frequency—which rarely happens with a traditional business book that is read by a limited number of people. Thus far, all the experiments have shown promising results.

When an early reader was asked what he thought the book accomplished, he wrote:

For someone who has overseen several deliberate change initiatives...

- The book puts a smile on your face.

- It makes you appreciate how the structure of the story logically lays out the change process along with typical obstacles.

- It forces you to remember how much common sense is involved and how predictable some of the process steps are—but that relationships, patience, and COMMUNICATION should never be underestimated, and that change is emotional.

- It shows you a low-threat tool that can be used to initiate discussion around the process for newly assembled project teams. The ability to refer back to a humorous account of a change process like this can defuse some of the emotion experienced by teams that periodically get caught up in what they think only they are experiencing.

- It provides a tool to stimulate discussion, around innovation, throughout an organization. Inevitably, the lifecycle brings you to stagnation and complacency. Why not throw an iceberg in front of a few folks every now and then?

For someone who hasn't led or participated in a pragmatic change initiative...

- It puts a smile on your face because you can identify with one or several of the penguins right away.

- It gives you a quick but also comprehensive picture of a methodical (and familiar) change initiative in a digestible format.

- It helps you see yourself as one of the heroes and envision yourself as an eligible champion for change—because it allows you to decipher the mysteries of what you may have previously thought was territory reserved for only the bosses with all the answers.

- It shows that real progress requires the participation of a team, where everyone has an important role (including you) and everyone knows his role.

- And in all cases—those who have been through a major change effort, those who have not, those at the top of enterprises, and those who are not—the book helps create new and better skills, and (most importantly) new and better results.

That's not a bad summary of our intentions.

The Authors

John Kotter is the leadership and change guru at Harvard Business School. He is the author of eleven books that have been honored or have become business bestsellers. Professor Kotter gives speeches and seminars at Harvard and around the world. He lives in Cambridge, Massachusetts, with wife Nancy Dearman, daughter Caroline, and son Jonathan.

Holger Rathgeber is the modern global manager. He works for Becton Dickinson, one of the world's leading medical technology companies. Rathgeber is from Frankfurt, Germany. He spent his first professional years in Asia. Since 2004, he has lived in White Plains, New York, with wife Jutta and sons Daniel and Benny.